Finding Freedom
Through Forgiveness!

Pastor Steve Eden

DEDICATION

I would like to dedicate this book to My Lord and
Savior Jesus Christ as well as the late E. Stanley Jones.
Both taught me the best way to overcome failure was to
let God use it for His purposes.

CONTENTS

Chapter 1:

Desperate For Relief

If you're reading this book, you may find yourself like so many others – grasping for any means necessary to experience a measure of healing and sanity from the tormenting emotions of resentment, unforgiveness, bitterness, and the like. You perhaps are seeking relief from the injustice of what someone did to you personally, or what someone did to a family member or loved one. Maybe you are trying to forgive yourself for something you did wrong years ago or even the pain you personally caused someone you love.

Nevertheless, you are keenly aware by now that your body, mind, and spirit are all pulling for you to find wholeness and wellness through any means necessary. Might I suggest, forgiveness?

One of the very first things you need to remember is we do not forgive because our salvation is at risk; we forgive because our health and peace of mind are at risk.

It was once said, "Resentment is like drinking poison but expecting the other person to die."

It was also said, "While we think in holding grudges we are harming others, the deepest harm is really to ourselves."

God, as revealed through Jesus Christ, is a loving Father who adores you whether you choose to forgive that person who hurt you or not. Yes, you heard me correctly! I just said God loves you whether you choose to forgive or not. He understands that forgiveness is much more for you than Him, and He has compassion for those held by the chains of bitterness.

This is very important for you to know because there is great empowerment in knowing God is with you in your battle to overcome poisonous emotions! He is not standing aloof somewhere waiting to cheer or boo you based on how you decide to proceed.

Our Bodies Are Moral-- Not Neutral

I have been on this planet for 46 years and I have discovered that forgiveness is not just imperative to a Christian's life, it is imperative to a human's life. As you probably know by now, you have ample opportunities to choose between forgiveness and holding a grudge. You will find yourself on both sides of this issue too: Those who've been injured and those who have caused injury to others.

The human body, in all of its incredible design, is made *BY* a moral God *FOR* morality. <u>Even an atheist cannot deny that our bodies are at home in attitudes of love, joy, peace, forgiveness, and good will.</u> On the other hand, our bodies begin to break down in attitudes of prolonged hate, worry, fear, resentment, and ill-will.

Dr. William Sadler said, "If we Americans would but walk in the love of God, half our diseases would fall off tomorrow and we would rise a new and healthy nation."

How can that be? Well, as a created being it has been written into us by our Creator/Designer how we function and operate the best. It is no different than the maker of an automobile designing a car to run on gasoline instead of milk. Optimum function is built into the car's design.

Could you imagine telling your doctor that you are going to take up hate and resentment as your new life attitudes? He would have you committed. Why? He may not know God, but He knows the damage not forgiving can write into your body and mind.

Where does this inner "payoff" towards forgiveness rather than resentments come from? It comes from your Creator, the One who designed you for Himself and His Nature.

One particular Sunday at Grace Church, I had a gentleman come up to me after a service and say, "I feel so free!" Guess what the Lord had just walked him through? Forgiving a co-worker! Notice he was free in forgiveness not bound. It's what He and his body are made for!

Opportunities To Get Offended

None of us can escape the fact that opportunities to be offended are going to come our way (Jesus mentions this in Luke 17:1). We live in a fallen world full of imperfect people. How long those people and their mistakes stay in our mind though; well, that is a different matter altogether.

Look at it this way: We cannot keep birds from flying over our head, but we can keep them from nesting in our hair for days on end. <u>It will always be OUR choice to respond right when we've been done wrong.</u>

What we want to make sure of is that something someone did to you 10 years ago is not still setting you back and causing a lack of peace in your mind today.

My Apologies…

I do want to take this time to say, "I am truly sorry for what happened to you. I am sorry for the time or times you got wounded and damaged; especially by someone close to you –

a parent, a relative, a child, or a spouse. I am so sorry you had to experience any kind of injustice, but the choice moving forward is yours. I admonish you as Paul did—to "let all bitterness and wrath be put away from you, along with all malice (your desire to injure someone)."

Ephesians 4:31-32 says, "Let all bitterness, wrath, anger, clamor, and evil speaking be put away from you, with all malice. 32 And be kind to one another, tenderhearted, <u>forgiving one another, just as God in Christ forgave you</u>."

The willingness to forgive is not just a sign of great maturity but great wisdom as well. Knowledge is knowing we should forgive, but wisdom is when we do.

You may say, "Pastor Steve, I know God desires me to forgive; I know it is the right thing to do, but why should I? Some people don't *deserve* my forgiveness, do they?" Great question. I'm so glad you asked!

Chapter 2

Why You Should Forgive: Divine Design

Many times having the "why" answered to some of life's difficult questions can provide the strength we need to act on what the Lord is *asking* us to do, but maybe our emotions don't always *want* to do. This chapter covers the very first and foremost reason you should choose the freedom and power of forgiveness:

1) Bitterness is not your divine design.

In chapter one, I touched on the fact our bodies were made by a moral God *for* morality. Let's go deeper and uncover some amazing truths about our inner workings.

1 Corinthians 6:13 says, "The body is for the Lord and the Lord is for the body."

It is very important to understand your body and mind are made FOR God. They thrive in His character, attitudes, and code of conduct.

You feel and function better when you love your enemies, choose joy despite your circumstances, and forgive instead of grudge on someone. Why? You're made in the image of a forgiving God who is and does all those very same things. What looks good on Him always looks good on you! You've heard milk does a body good, but it has nothing on forgiveness!!

Ill-will Versus Good Will

Bitterness, resentment, and revenge may be fuel, but they are definitely not the fuel you are made for! Imagine putting orange juice in your car instead of gasoline. It will cause great harm to your vehicle because when it was created, your car was *designed* to run on gasoline not on orange juice.

In the same way, as human beings whose bodies are made "for the Lord," we are not made for "ILL-WILL" but for good will. Goodwill has much more return and useable energy for us than grudges.

There may not be anything more unnatural, unsatisfying, or unhealthy for you than resentments, bitterness, and ill-will.

There is a reason the first half of the word ill-will is "ILL." If you hang out too long in it, it can make you very sick.

One doctor told the late missionary E. Stanley Jones, "I know of no single thing that wreaks more havoc on the human body than hidden resentments."

Gas goes in the car. Oil goes in the lamp. Christ and His Spirit go in the human being. This is the law of divine design.

Purpose and function always precede design. No one makes a car and then steps back and says, "Well, I wonder what that is for? I wonder how it works? What shall we put in it to make it go?" They had all those questions answered **_before_** they began making the car!

I can assure you God didn't make you and handcraft you in your mother's womb with no idea what fulfills you or how you are designed to function! No, God made you with purpose and function in mind and that is to know Him intimately and reflect Him. When you do, His expression is life, health, and fuel to you.

9

Colossians 1:16-17 says, "For in Him (Christ) all things were created: things in heaven and on earth, visible and invisible, whether thrones or powers or rulers or authorities; all things have been created through Him and <u>FOR Him.</u> 17 He is before all things, and <u>in Him all things hold together.</u>

Notice how everything is "held together" by Him! <u>Societies, nations, families, you name it-- are all held together by Christ, His principles, and His attitudes.</u> I challenge any politician or government official to try and build a society or nation on principles and attitudes opposite of what Jesus Christ taught, because they will not hold together.

How about a society built on dishonesty? It would rot in fear and the absence of trust. How about a city or nation built on selfishness? It would rot with competition and greed and the absence of benevolence, togetherness, and compassion. How about a family or marriage built on unforgiveness? They have no chance of survival because it is the character and virtues of Christ that hold all things together.

<u>Scriptural Proof We Are Made For Christ:</u>

In Matthew 22, the Pharisees tried to trick Jesus as to whether people should be loyal to Him or to Caesar. They asked Jesus if it was right to pay taxes. Check out His response.

Matthew 22:18-21 says, "But Jesus, knowing their evil intent, said, "You hypocrites, why are you trying to trap me? 19 Show me the coin used for paying the tax." They brought him a denarius, 20 And Jesus said to them, "Whose image and inscription is this?" 21 They said to Him, "Caesar's." And He said to them, "<u>Render therefore to Caesar whatever has Caesar's image on it, and to God what has His image on it</u>."

There is a stunning principle and truth here. Jesus is revealing that what belongs to God, what came from Him, and what has His image fastened upon it, must be given back to God. This is why without exception every human being that surrenders to God is fulfilled in that moment. They do not become a slave, they become free, for they have just surrendered to the One for which they were made.

Another great example is found in Mark 5. Here is a man under the rule of darkness – specifically under the rule of a demon named "Legion."

Mark 5:5 says, "And always, night and day, he was in the mountains and in the tombs, crying out and cutting himself with stones."

This man is not thriving under the rule of darkness, as evidenced by the fact he cuts himself with stones trying to displace and nullify his internal pain. He also cries all day and night. Yet look what happens after He surrenders to Christ.

Mark 5:15 says, "Then they came to Jesus, and saw the one who had been demon-possessed and had the legion: sitting, clothed, and in his right mind."

After this man's encounter with Christ and His righteous rule, the people found him seated, clothed, and in his RIGHT mind! Not in his wrong mind, not in his neutral mind, but in his RIGHT mind. He had been set right in Christ.

John 1:3-4 says, "All things were made through Him, and without Him nothing was made that was made. 4 In Him (Christ) was life, and the life was the light of men."

Notice in Christ was life and His life is the LIGHT of men! His life, virtues, and character do not dim us or darken us; they heighten us. Walking in the forgiveness of Christ lights me rather than dims me. Releasing people who have wronged me heals me; it doesn't harm me.

1 John 5:3 says, "This is the love of God that we keep His commands, and His commands are not burdensome."

I will never forget the day that I discovered God's commands were not ultimatums for me to "do or else," but rather loving instruction from the One who designed me and my body for His nature.

Our Father's command to release those who have injured us and to "forgive as we've been forgiven" is His loving guidance for us because He knows our inner workings so well.

Everything in your design backs you obeying your Father's loving instruction because He made you for Himself. Nothing in your design backs you operating in hatred, selfishness, anxiety, or revenge. When God made us, He put within us "a way," and that way is the way of Jesus.

This is verified and supported by Romans 8:29 which says each of us are "predestined to be conformed to the image of Christ."

Name one of the principles or attitudes Jesus taught that is not life giving or health producing. The history of man bears out that when we work His way we work well; when we work some other way we tend to work our own demise.

As I stated before, our bodies are not neutral, they are moral. Recently I was visiting with an atheist who is actually an acquaintance of mine. He told me, "People in this world don't have to be Christians to do good;" to which I told him I totally agreed. Then I asked, "But why would you even want to do good if there is no God? Why would it matter?" He responded, "*Because it feels good to do good.*"

To which I agreed again and then asked, "Why does it feel good inside when a human does good? Where does that very clear mental, physical, and emotional payoff come from?" He just smiled and shifted awkwardly; he did not have an answer.

You and I both know, the presence of this embedded moral code came from the God who made us in His moral image. What are the odds that this moral payoff written into us was passed onto us by a shrew or a monkey in the evolutionary process? Uh, I think not.

One physician told E. Stanley Jones, "The Kingdom of God is in the tissues of man. Christ's way is the healthy way."

Proverbs 14:30 says, "A sound and peaceful heart is life to the body, but envy rots your bones."

Our bones produce the cells of our immune system so we actually resist disease more effectively when we keep our emotions free from envy. We also see that a heart full of peace, not strife and worry, blesses and gives life to our body.

The God's Word Translation of Proverbs 4:20-23 says, "My son, pay attention to my words. <u>Open your ears to what I say. 21 Do not lose sight of these things. Keep them deep within your heart 22 because they are life to those who find them and they heal the whole body.</u> 23 Guard your heart more than anything else, because the source of your life flows from it."

Verse 22 says God's Word is "life" to you and "healing to your whole body." The Living Bible translation says, "God's Word is radiant health to you!" Psalm 107:20 adds, "He sent His word and <u>healed us</u>."

I realize the yoga booty ballet machine can help keep you robust, healthy, and in shape on the outside but clearly God's Word does great work on the inside! Why work out the outer man but never give any thought to the inner man?

Proverbs 17:22 says, "A merry heart (laughter) does good like medicine, but a broken spirit dries the bones."

Again we see a divine design written into us that produces built-in bodily rewards.

Proverbs 3:7-8 says, "Do not be wise in your own eyes, fear the Lord and depart from evil, <u>for it will be health to your flesh and strength to your bones."</u>

Wow, our departure from evil is health to us and strength to our bones! Thank God for the presence of His clear embedded moral code.

The Amplified Bible in Matthew 11:28-30 quotes Jesus saying, "Come to Me, all who are weary and heavily burdened [by religious rituals that provide no peace], and I will give you rest [refreshing your souls with salvation]. 29 Take My yoke upon you and learn from Me [following Me as My disciple], for I am gentle and humble in heart, and you will find rest (renewal, blessed quiet) for your souls. 30 For My yoke is easy [to bear] and My burden is light."

We are perfectly designed for the yoke of Christ. He describes our joining and partnership with Him, which is what a yoke is—as restful, easy, and light. I can testify to this-- walking in His character always feels like wings, not like weights.

Bitterness Defiles, Not Delights

The definition of bitterness is: Resentment or anger, hostile toward, unpleasantly cold or offended.

None of those sound too life-giving. One Doctor said, "Bitterness eats like acid into our moral and physical nature."

Hebrews 12:15 says, "Be careful lest anyone fall short of the grace of God; <u>lest any root of bitterness springing up cause trouble, for by this many have become defiled...</u>"

This passage says by the root of bitterness many are defiled and corrupted, not blessed or fulfilled. This again is why our Father's loving instruction is to forgive those who we believe have wronged us; it is life to us.

One struggling pastor who had been deeply wounded by a congregant said, "Father, I see the absolute necessity of getting rid of all this bitterness-- for if I live with my hate, I can't seem to live with myself. I surrender myself and my emotions to you."

Is there a more telling statement than, "If I live with my hate, I can't live with myself?"

As human beings we definitely pass on to our bodies the health or unhealth of our minds. <u>Some in the medical industry today say as much as 80% of all human structural disease originates in our thoughts, attitudes, and emotions.</u>

Once again, it is worth saying while we think in holding resentments we are harming others, the deepest harm is really to ourselves.

The bottom line is, as human beings we are not made for a root of bitterness. You are too great a creation to be satisfied by it. Bitterness is sand in your human machinery, yet love is oil. These are the facts. You didn't make yourself so you cannot change this about yourself. You work better with the oil of love than with the sand of hate. So when we choose to harbor a grudge, we not only sin against God, we sin against our own bodies, emotions, and minds.

Even if you asked an atheist doctor, who doesn't believe God exists but understands the human body and its function, he would agree

Christ like attitudes are healthy attitudes, and will produce the healing you long for!

Chapter 3:

Why You Should Forgive:
All The Other Reasons

Aside from Chapter 2's first and most important reason you should forgive—your divine design; there are a host of other reasons the Holy Spirit inside you desires to walk you down the path of forgiveness that produces freedom! Let's explore those:

2) To be released from the tormentors.

The Webster's dictionary defines **torment** as: Extreme pain, anguish in the body or mind, to cause to suffer.

Oh the people I've seen suffer at the hands of bitterness, ill-will, hatred, and unforgiveness! Far too many have been plunged into a "victim mentality," allowing the pains others have caused them to lord over them long after the initial transgression.

In Matthew chapter 18, Jesus tells the story of a king and his servant which gives us some insight into the torment of unforgiveness. The king had forgiven the servant of a tremendous debt (around the equivalent of $1,000,000 today). Yet the servant, because he evidently did not *believe* the king's word that his debt was forgiven, went and choked a man who owed him around the equivalent of $20 today. In the end, Jesus points out the reality of how people who do not forgive face the torment of that choice. Here is the passage:

Matthew 18:21-35 says, "Then Peter came to Jesus and said, "Lord, how often shall my brother sin against me, and I forgive him? Up to seven times?" 22 Jesus said to him, "I do not say to you, up to seven times, but up to seventy times seven. 23 Therefore the kingdom of heaven is like a certain king who wanted to settle accounts with his servants. 24 And when he had begun to settle accounts, one was brought to him who owed him ten thousand talents. 25 But as he was not able to pay, his master commanded that he be sold, with his wife and children and all that he had, and that payment be made.

26 The servant therefore fell down before him, saying, 'Master, have patience with me, and I will pay you all.' 27 Then the master of that servant was moved with compassion, released him, and forgave him the debt. 28 "But that servant went out and found one of his fellow servants who owed him a hundred denarii; and he laid hands on him and took him by the throat, saying, 'Pay me what you owe!' 29 So his fellow servant fell down at his feet and begged him, saying, 'Have patience with me, and I will pay you all.' 30 And he would not, but went and threw him into prison till he should pay the debt. 31 So when his fellow servants saw what had been done, they were very grieved, and came and told their master all that had been done. 32 Then his master, after he had called him, said to him, 'You wicked servant! I forgave you all that debt because you begged me. 33 <u>Should you not also have had compassion on your fellow servant, just as I had pity on you?</u>' 34 And his master was angry, and delivered him to the <u>tormentors</u> until he should pay all that was due to him. 35 "So My heavenly Father also will do to you if each of you, from his heart, does not forgive his brother his trespasses."

I believe because the human body and mind is moral not neutral, God doesn't intentionally punish everyone in unforgiveness because unforgiveness is its own punishment. Notice the end result of the man's unwillingness to forgive lands him in a place of "torment."

It's so interesting to recognize the core of the wicked servant's unforgiveness was his own unbelief. He didn't really believe the king had forgiven his debt or it would have shown up in how willing he was to forgive others. Accepting that we are forgiven is a primary key to forgiveness, because we cannot give away something we don't think we have.

It should be noted that Jesus did teach aspects of the Old Testament law before He shed His blood for the remission of our sin. He would take opportunity to "raise the bar" of even the law's requirements so Israel could SEE their need for a Savior/Helper.

For example, in Matthew 5:27-28 Jesus said, "You have heard that it was said, 'You shall not commit adultery.' 28 But I say to you that whoever looks at a woman to lust for her has already committed adultery with her in his heart." Notice He actually raises the command!

That is what He is doing here in Matthew 18 by telling them in Verse 35 if they don't forgive others, His Heavenly Father cannot forgive them. This should not be used as a "threat" to born again, Christ filled Christians to "forgive or else." Let me explain why.

Everything in the Old Covenant shifts from a "demand" to God's "supply" in the New Covenant. In other words, in the New Covenant, once Jesus shed His blood for the remission of sin, God is not saying, "Forgive or I won't forgive you…" He says, "Forgive because I have now supplied you with the forgiveness to forgive with." It's very similar to the principle of 1 John 4:19 which is also in the New Covenant-- "We love because *HE FIRST LOVED* us."

There is no post-cross teaching of the Father not forgiving people who do not forgive others. Every reference is "forgive as Christ forgave you." See, for example, Colossians 3:13 and Ephesians 4:32.

This puts New Testament believers exactly where Christ wants them: Under His law of supply, not the old law of demand. He desires to supply everything we need to carry out the commands of God. If we love because God first loved us then it is as easy to say we forgive because God first forgave us. This "law of supply" is at the core of the New Covenant God initiated through Christ's blood and empowers us to stay free from the "tormentors."

3) To prevent Satan from taking advantage of you.

2 Corinthians 2:10-11 says, "Now whom you forgive anything, I also forgive. For if indeed I have forgiven anything, I have forgiven that one for your sakes in the presence of Christ, 11 lest Satan should take advantage of us; for we are not ignorant of his devices."

Paul tells the church at Corinth that Satan takes advantage of us through unforgiveness. It is one of his main devices and weapons.

Our enemy likes to tell us, "Hold onto your grudges and your hate; that will give you power over those that hurt you by hurting them." All the while, that is how he takes power over you and hurts you instead.

The enemy wants to destroy you by asking you to take something into your heart, mind, and body that God never intended to be there. It's a trap, it's bait, it's a snare; and yet so many well meaning, even mature believers, fall into it.

Offense Is A Trap!

The Greek word for offense in the New Testament is "skandalon." It means a trap, a snare, a stumbling block. So Satan says, "You have the right to be offended. You have the right to take revenge. Here, drink this poison and we can watch *them* die." Then he steps back waiting for all that ill-will and anger to bring death to you instead.

Someone asked an alcoholic husband why he got drunk all the time. He answered, "It's the only way I have of getting even with my wife for what she did to me four years ago."

Talk about being deceived! She hurt him four years ago and he relives it everyday in a mix of alcohol, ego, and self pity. I know we don't put degrees on sin, but couldn't carrying all that anger and "paying her back" for four years be a greater transgression than her original mistake? It is at least worth considering. He will have a hard time finding healing when he reopens his old wound everyday with a tall glass of revenge. God wants to heal Him; God has provided the way, but will he be humble enough to receive it? Otherwise, the enemy continues taking advantage of him.

4) To be effective in the present.

The fourth and final reason you should forgive is so you don't get locked in the wrong time zone!

In Philippians 3:12-14 Paul says, "Not that I have already attained, or am already perfected; but I press on, that I may lay hold of that for which Christ Jesus has also laid hold of me. 13 Brethren, I do not count myself to have apprehended; but one thing I do, forgetting those things which are behind and reaching forward to those things which are ahead, 14 I press toward the goal for the prize of the upward call of God in Christ Jesus."

Paul, having murdered Christians at one time, had a lot to forget and leave behind; but here he refuses to allow the enemy to keep him locked in his past.

One thing about bitterness, it can absolutely freeze you in the past and thus render you ineffective in the present. It can affect how you go forward towards all God has for you. It can affect your demeanor towards your family, spouse, and children. If you won't allow God to heal you for your own sake, please let Him heal you for your family and children's sake.

There's just too much to live for, to be thankful for, and too much good ahead in your life to live in the past. Paul says the high call of God awaits you as well as laying hold of the whole reason Christ laid hold of you! Make sure you don't let one mistake you or someone else made become a thousand times greater by rehashing it every day.

You simply cannot go down life's highway using only the rearview mirror. You will miss all that is right in front of you plus you might run over a few people as well.

Pastor Steve Eden

Chapter 4:

What Forgiveness Actually Is

If we are going to walk in the absolute freedom God promises through forgiveness, it is imperative that we truly know and understand what forgiveness is. There are a lot of theories in Christianity and the American culture as to what it means to forgive someone.

For example, the idea that "forgiving is forgetting" is cruel. There are some things that we have done and/or that have been done to us that the enemy will never let us forget; so to equate forgiving with forgetting is a train wreck waiting to happen. The following should help you grow in your understanding though:

1) Forgiveness is the releasing of a debt.

Think of the terminology, "You <u>owe</u> me $20," or "You <u>owe</u> me an apology." They are rooted in the idea that a debt has been incurred.

31

Therefore, forgiveness by definition is "the releasing of a debt." It is not saying what the other person did was right or OK by any means, it simply is saying they don't "owe" you for it.

The beautiful part about releasing the debt someone owes you is it releases you too! It does release them but it also releases you from the pain, torment, and stress unforgiveness brings. Remember, those who hurt you were never made to be Lord of your heart and your character, Christ is. You are who you are regardless of whether they ever apologize or pay you back the money they owe you.

"Well, what about the debt I was owed?"

Forgiveness is acknowledging that Christ is your source and He more than "repays" whatever debt they incurred to you. In faith you are saying, "If you did not supply me the love you promised me, I do not walk away deficient in love, as Christ becomes the love you did not supply me!" Likewise you can say, "If you do not pay me the money you owe me, in the end, Christ is my Source and provision; not you."

The reason you can forgive is not rooted in some fairy tale pretending mechanism, Jesus really does make up the difference. This is why you don't roam the Earth a victim, but a victor! In Christ, you have more than enough of whatever somebody else has shorted you!

2) Forgiveness is a choice YOU make.

Forgiveness is not just the releasing of a debt, it is also a choice you make. One of our key missteps is after we get hurt we think that other person has the power to determine whether we forgive or not. We think, "Well, if they apologize I will forgive;" or "If they promise never to do it again, then I will forgive."

Since Christ is our source for forgiveness and not a person or apology, the choice to be better or to be bitter is ours. We don't have to wait on someone else's actions to determine our behavior. We are who we are in Christ regardless of the actions and attitudes of others.

The power to forgive doesn't come from an apology it comes from Christ! The power to forgive is already in you through Christ!

Deuteronomy 30:19 says, "I have put life and death before you, therefore CHOOSE life."

It does not say God chooses for you, the devil chooses for you, Uncle Joe chooses for you, or your ex-spouse chooses for you; you choose.

Notice it says "Choose life so you AND your descendants can live." A root of bitterness doesn't affect only you, it can affect all those around you. If it's true as someone said, "Whoever nurses resentment nurses a cobra," then why would you bring that thing into your house? It could wreak havoc on your kids, your spouse, or even yes, your family pet!

3) Forgiveness is Supernatural!

True forgiveness comes from God, not from a human being! You've heard it said, "To err is human but to forgive is divine..." That is so true.

So many people have said, "Pastor Steve, I just cannot forgive that person. I am hurt so badly." That is a true statement-- in and of themselves they cannot forgive, but I promise you, if they can *receive* all the Lord's forgiveness He has for them, they will be empowered to forgive others!

Romans 8:11 says, "The same Spirit that raised Christ from the dead lives in you…" so if God's Spirit can raise the dead I know He can empower you to forgive.

The testimony of the New Covenant over and over again is that Christ is our Source for life and Godliness. We forgive because He FIRST forgave us. We are kind to others because He FIRST demonstrated His kindness to us.

In John 13:34 Jesus said, "A new command I give to you-- that you love one another AS I HAVE LOVED YOU."

Jesus is revealing the same concept in John 15:5 when He stated, "I am the Vine, you are the branches. He who abides in Me and I in Him bears much fruit for without Me you can do nothing." In other words, I am your Source and Supply for whatever you have need of.

Being a branch means – if you can receive, you can forgive!

The first thing a child has to learn is to receive from its mother. If the child can receive, it can live. We are no different as children of God. If we can receive, we can live, bear, and manifest fruit from Jesus constant supply!

Most Christians unfortunately try to forgive out of a sense of duty rather from God's Grace they have received. <u>Duty is enslaving as it is a perceived response to a demand God has, while God's Grace is empowering because it comes from all Christ our Vine is supplying.</u>

4) Forgiveness is free.

Forgiveness is free but trust is earned. Why do you think it's called for**give**ness and not for**sale**ness? When you go around putting conditions on everyone else as to whether you are going to forgive or not, it is definitely forsaleness!

Keep this in mind: Forgiveness is not just a gift you get to give someone else, it is a gift you get to give yourself!! It's like going to the furniture store and buying a recliner for someone but then finding out you also get one for yourself for free!

Beware of the "IF" factor. It says, "IF you suffer enough… IF you apologize enough… IF you promise to, "never do it again" enough…" then I will forgive you. No, forgiveness is a gift you get to give someone else because it comes from God not from human behavior."

You say, "Well this is just not fair!" I agree! You are so right that so much in life is not fair. It's not fair that Christ's Spirit is living inside of you and me right now! It's not fair we are reconciled to God! It's not fair we have His Word, His Person, His Presence, and His Name; you're right there's a lot in life that's not fair! We are benefactors of so many things that aren't fair when you think about it. It's always a good perspective to acknowledge we have not always gotten what we deserved.

Luke 23:33-34 reads, "When they came to the place called Calvary, they crucified Jesus there, along with the criminals—one on his right, the other on his left. 34 Jesus said, "Father, forgive them, for they do not know what they do."

These people were mocking Him, sneering at Him, and yet there is no forsaleness here; just heartfelt forgiveness. Could you imagine Jesus asking someone to please apologize to Him so He could be empowered to forgive them?

In Acts 7:60, we see the same Spirit in Christ now forgiving in and through Stephen.

Acts 7:60 says, "Then Stephen fell on his knees and cried out, "Lord, do not hold this sin against them." When he had said this, he fell asleep."

It is truly amazing how the same Spirit that forgave the soldiers at Christ's cross is now forgiving Stephen's murderers! We see once again there is no apology offered and thus no *condition* upon the forgiveness; it's free.

5) Forgiveness is your opportunity to give to another what God has given you!!

I know we don't like to hear that; but what if that wound you received has just given you the opportunity to share with someone else a gift God has shared with you? Isn't that what we pray for daily -- "God, when others see me I pray they see you!" Then why when people treat us wrong or hurt us do we whine and complain instead of thanking God for a wonderful opportunity to reveal His character?

When your spouse says to you, "I am so sorry for what I did…" you can respond with, "I forgive you because you've given me the opportunity to share with you what God has given so many times to me. I pray you not only see my forgiveness in this, but God's forgiveness as well."

What beauty to experience the reality and power of forgiveness, which is that it heals two ways – when you get it AND when you give it!

Pastor Steve Eden

Chapter 5:

5 Myths About Forgiveness

Now that I've told you what forgiveness is, I want to tell you what it's not! There are a handful of myths regarding forgiveness that have bound far too many people.

Myth #1: If you don't trust them, you didn't forgive them.

Is there a myth that has brought more confusion than this one? Someone might have said, "Well if you forgave me, why don't you trust me? Or why don't you let me back into your life?"

John 2:23-24 (NLT)– Because of the miraculous signs Jesus did in Jerusalem at the Passover celebration, many began to trust in Him. 24 <u>But Jesus didn't trust them</u>, because He knew all about people.

In the New King James Version of John 2:24 it records, "But Jesus did not commit Himself to them, because He knew all men." We know Jesus did not walk around with unforgiveness in His heart towards anyone, yet the Bible does record He didn't trust or fully commit Himself to certain people. Why? He's full of wisdom.

Forgiveness is free but trust is earned. If I hire a babysitter to watch my son and she abuses him physically, I can and should forgive her but does that mean I should ask her to come back tomorrow? I don't think so! Wisdom does come into play in the life of any believer.

If someone asks me later if they should use that sitter to babysit their kids, do I lie? No, but I don't nurse, rehearse, and disperse offense either. I simply speak the truth of my experience to them; and I do it without bias or grudge.

It's the same principle if you go into business with someone and they take some of your profit and prove they are not trustworthy. Should you forgive? Absolutely, but it does not mean you jump right back into business with them again.

Life experience teaches us to build healthy boundaries around certain people, that is wisdom. Be careful though, that you don't build healthy grudges around people instead.

I had a friend I played basketball with and during one of our devotion times he said to me, "So if a guy's wife keeps cheating on him he's supposed to just forgive her and keep trusting her?" I said those are two different questions with two different answers. The first answer is yes and the second is no. He should forgive her for his own peace of mind and health. Trusting her is a whole different issue. Can he work back towards a place of trust some day?—possibly, if his wife decides she wants to save the marriage.

Myth #2: Forgiveness is a feeling.

This centers around the idea, "Well if I don't feel like I've forgiven, then I haven't; or if I still have negative emotions toward that individual, I must not have forgiven them."

I have long held the thought that our feelings are not even close to being the best discerner of truth and reality. Even though we don't always feel righteous, are we? Yes. Even if we don't always feel God's love, does He love us? Of course. Let's be honest: Forgiveness doesn't always "feel" great (especially at first, when the wound is fresh). Releasing the debt can be instant, but the healing of our emotions is often a process!

My wife Stacy has forgiven me of many things through the years, but some of those things took a little bit longer for the hurt to be healed.

You may experience old emotions from a wound years later simply through a TV show or something you hear in a song. That does NOT mean you have not forgiven that person! It just means you had a wound there from before and it may still be in the process of healing.

When old feelings arise we first counter with, "I have forgiven and I have released that person's debt; and I thank you Father, for continuing to heal me. I surrender myself and any negative emotions to you."

With that as my response, I have found each day the process gets a little bit easier. The key is don't ignore old emotions or stuff them away; counter them with prayer.

Secondly, don't let the devil convince you that you have not forgiven just because you experience some familiar emotion from the past or get "triggered" by something.

Myth #3: If you don't forgive others then God can't forgive you.

This one has been used by well-meaning Christians against well-meaning Christians for years! Of course, the enemy has also used this one against many of us-- trying to deceive us into self-effort and earning forgiveness from God.

I alluded to this concept previously, but there is no post-cross doctrine that tells us as Christians we can only be forgiven IF we forgive others.

Jesus, before He died on the cross, still taught certain concepts of the law in order to continue to point mankind to their need for a Savior. This is because the New Covenant doesn't really begin until the shedding of His blood. Hebrews 9:18 says no one initiates a covenant without the shedding of blood. So the New Covenant didn't begin on a certain page of your Bible, it began when Jesus shed His blood.

So in Matthew 18, when Jesus said "if you don't forgive others from your heart, your Heavenly Father won't forgive you..." that was not so we would all say, "Wow I am an incredible forgiver! God has to forgive me!" It was designed for us to say, "Oh God, please help me; I need your power and grace to forgive. I need your heart to forgive completely because my heart doesn't want to."

In Matthew 18:33 Jesus gives a glimpse into the New Covenant He would be initiating:

He says, "Shouldn't you have had mercy on your fellow servant, just as I had mercy on you?"

He is revealing the way of the New Covenant to come. He is saying, "This is where we are going – I will show you mercy, and out of that which you receive from Me, you can show mercy to others." This is a much "easier yoke" than, "you guys better forgive or else..."

Religious duty is trying to forgive from a perceived demand God has, while Grace is forgiving through the empowering supply of Christ!

Let us visit once again all the passages of Scripture that detail the post-cross doctrine of "Forgive out of the forgiveness that has been supplied to you by Christ Himself!"

Colossians 2:13 says, "And you, being dead in your trespasses and the uncircumcision of your flesh, He has made alive together with Him, <u>having forgiven you all trespasses…</u>"

Colossians 3:13 says, "bearing with one another, and forgiving one another, if anyone has a complaint against another; <u>even as Christ forgave you…</u>"

1 John 2:12 says, "I write to you, little children, <u>because your sins are forgiven you for His name's sake.</u>"

Ephesians 4:32 says, "And be kind to one another, tenderhearted, forgiving one another, <u>just as God in Christ forgave you.</u>"

Hebrews 10:17-18 says, "God adds, "Their sins and their lawless deeds I will remember no more." 18 <u>Now where there is remission of these, there is no longer an offering for sin.</u>"

In the New Covenant, it is imperative you understand that God is not holding your forgiveness hostage from you until you earn it, deserve it, merit it, or occasion it!

We know the testimony of the New Covenant is that God's love is free not earned, and God's righteousness is free not earned; so why would forgiveness be different? When Christ came inside of you to live forever, why would He not bring with Him total forgiveness? Would He actually say, "I know you have Me living in you, but you'll have to work for My forgiveness." The fact He's living inside you is proof He has eradicated your sin issue and atoned for all your sin!

This is a good spot to clarify God's forgiveness and glorious salvation are indeed incredibly amazing, but they MUST BE received. These passages we have looked at in this chapter are not saying everyone on the planet is saved and/or forgiven but the offer certainly has been made available for everyone. According to Acts 26:17-18 and John 1:12, what God has offered must be "received" by us.

In Acts 26:17-18 Jesus says, " I will deliver you from the *Jewish* people, as well as *from* the Gentiles, to whom I now send you, 18 to open their eyes, *in order* to turn *them* from darkness to light, and *from* the power of Satan to God, <u>that they may receive forgiveness of sins</u> and an inheritance among those who are sanctified by faith in Me."

John 1:12 says, "But as many as <u>received Him</u>, to them He gave the right to become children of God, to those who believe in His name."

<u>Myth #4: You have not forgiven until you've forgotten.</u>

This is simply a very cruel statement. If someone is molested by their step dad or by an uncle; that is simply not just going to vanish from their mind.

Now can they be healed from their pain? Can God redeem what happened and use it for His glory, for their good, and for the good of others? Absolutely.

I counseled a woman who was molested as a little girl who asked God for years, "Where were you?" When she reached age 40, she again found herself asking the Lord about what happened and she heard Him say to her, "I was there. What he did to you, he did to Me because I am in you." The Lord added, "I am not a victim and neither are you – we are going to use this to help a lot of young women overcome molestation! I am going to turn your sorrow into a song!"

<u>All suffering and injustice loses it's shame when it becomes useable. Look at Jesus – He didn't just bear the cross, HE USED THE CROSS. He turned what was a demonstration of man's hate into a revelation of God's love!</u>

Jesus has the ability to turn all human pain into possibility! He can turn any crucifixion into an Easter Sunrise if we place it in His redemptive hands.

One of my favorite authors, E. Stanley Jones once said, "The Christian is safe because he can not only stand everything that happens to him; he can use everything that happens to him."

<u>Sometimes God keeps us from trials and tribulations, but sometimes we get to use them to help others. Everything furthers us as Christians</u>. Every event, positive or negative, becomes an opportunity in our hands if we allow our Heavenly Father to teach us how to use it.

Who wants to be a victim their whole life? Who wants to blame every person and circumstance outside of us for our lack of freedom and happiness? Those days are gone. I refuse to let my joy be in someone else's hands.

Someone is going to possess our memory; either God or the devil, so I say we let God have our memories and use them for good.

Myth #5- You must confess every sin you commit in order to be forgiven.

This myth comes from what I believe has been a misinterpretation of the passage 1 John 1:9 which says, "If we confess our sins, He is faithful and just to forgive us our sins and to cleanse us from all unrighteousness."

<u>There are two types of Christians on the planet:</u>

Those who have received all of God's forgiveness through the body and blood of Jesus Christ and are therefore at rest, happy, and thankful. Then there are those who are making installment payments to God so they can be forgiven.

There are those who have received by faith the full measure of Christ's forgiveness; and there are those who have only received partial forgiveness and are working for the rest.

There are those who know they are forgiven and there are those who don't.

<u>We are cleansed and brought into right relationship with God either through what Christ did or by what we do; it cannot be both.</u> Either we are forgiven or there is work to be done to ensure our forgiveness; it cannot be both.

Fortunately, God uses a blood based economy for forgiveness, not a confession based or apology based, or an "I promise never to do that again" based economy.

I really believe Christians would be a lot better at forgiveness if they truly knew all their sins had been paid in full by Christ.

There is such benefit to knowing you are actually forgiven because of what Christ has done on your behalf. For one, it gives you a place of security to grow from in your relationship with your Heavenly Father. From the natural realm, we know plants that are secure in their soil grow much better than plants that are constantly uprooted and starting over.

Another benefit is now you have all the power and resource of God to overcome all bitterness and offense that tries to come your way! You can give forgiveness because you've actually received it!

1 John 1:9 was never intended to be our daily routine to extract or merit forgiveness from God. It was never meant to take the place of Jesus' blood. It was never intended to be a burdensome command from God.

Jesus is not a vendor of religious goods and services making His forgiveness, love, and righteousness separate from Himself. No, when you got Him, you received all He is and all He offers! Not just in theory, but in reality and experience!

Let's read 1 John 1:8-10 and unpack it.

1 John 1:8-10 says, "If we say that we have no sin, we deceive ourselves, and the truth is not in us. 9 If we confess our sins, He is faithful and just to forgive us our sins and to cleanse us from all unrighteousness. 10 If we say that we have not sinned, we make Him a liar, and His word is not in us."

Looking at verse 8, how many born again children of God do you know who are not aware they have sinned? I don't know of any. So is it not very possible, John is talking about unbelievers here?

Isn't it possible there were unbelievers in the churches back then like there are today? Or do we assume everyone who walks into the doors of a church are saved? I don't.

One theory is that John is addressing early Gnostics in the church who claimed to be without sin and that sin was not even real (because that was what Gnostics believed). They believed life only existed in the spiritual and that the natural realm did not matter.

John is possibly saying, "Instead of believing there is no sin, how about you own up to it; acknowledge yours, and receive Jesus' cleansing from not just one sin but from ALL UNRIGHTEOUSNESS!

John never says to confess our sin so God can cleanse us from that "one sin;" he says God cleanses us from ALL unrighteousness. That sounds like the offer of the new birth to me!

Whichever way you interpret 1 John 1:9, the problem is if we go confessing all our sin so we can be forgiven, what happens if we forget one? Even the most prideful person wouldn't dare say they have remembered and confessed every single sin they have ever committed. This leads to great insecurity, and insecurity stunts growth.

The truth is we didn't even become a sinner because we committed a sin, we were born into sin because of Adam. That's why Jesus said you must be BORN AGAIN to get "born" out of sin.

Now, let me be clear, I certainly "confess my sin" to Jesus each time I fail and am made aware of it by the Holy Spirit. I do not confess it though SO I WILL BE FORGIVEN, I confess it because Jesus and I are in an intimate relationship and He is my best friend. My wife Stacy and I are married and when I mess up I fess up because, like Christ, we are in an intimate relationship together.

We should never take the honesty out of any relationship correct? <u>The positional truth is I am forgiven before God in Christ, but the relational truth is that when I blow it I apologize to my Husband and Best Friend Jesus.</u> I experience cleansing and healing in my mind, soul, and body (because my *spirit* was already made clean the day I was born again and Christ moved in)!

Understanding just how forgiven you are by your Heavenly Father is huge because it is His forgiveness to you that can now come THROUGH you. It is that forgiveness that breaks the power of bitterness and offense.

Chapter 6:

Diagnosing Symptoms of Unforgiveness:

In battling one of Satan's biggest weapons against our health and peace of mind, it is important we are able to recognize signs and symptoms of unforgiveness, ill-will, or offense. I believe one way we can tell if we are harboring bitterness and in need of our Father's healing is to answer the following questions:

1) Do you have lingering anger towards someone?

Ephesians 4:28 says, "Be angry and yet do not sin. Don't let the sun go down on your anger."

It's ok to have anger, just beware of lingering anger. Even if your anger is "righteous" anger-- meaning it is based on an injustice done to another not your own personal wounded ego; if left to fester, it can corrode your soul into bitterness.

So many people, Christians and non Christians alike, hold onto anger and unforgiveness simply because they are waiting on the other person to apologize or make amends somehow. They act like the power to forgive is in the other person's hands.

Here is the cold hard truth: If you are waiting for an apology from someone in order to forgive them, don't hold your breath! That person may not even know they hurt you. They may not even know you're upset with them. Beyond that, they may know they hurt you and they may not care!

Do not be alarmed-- there is help and good news if that's the case. <u>The power to forgive doesn't come from an apology, it comes from Christ! Christ has supplied you with the power to forgive through His cross and His indwelling Spirit!</u>

There is no earthly reason that anyone else should have control over whether YOU forgive or not. It's always up to us to respond right when we've been done wrong. We are never to put our potential happiness, character, or well being in the hands of another person's behavior, attitude, or intentions.

I would go so far as to say if you are looking to someone else to make you happy or fulfill you; you are not loving them, you are using them. Remember, Jesus is your Vine, not them.

Could you imagine Jesus while on the cross asking someone to apologize to Him so He could finally say, "Father forgive them, they know not what they do?" He was able to forgive unilaterally, not waiting around for someone else to give Him a reason or even the power to forgive.

2) Do you rejoice at another's misfortune?

Do you hope an ex-spouse suffers terminal illness? Do you desire that great pain would come to someone who hurt your family? You can bet that if there is someone you are secretly or even openly hoping suffers calamity, disaster, or destruction, you have lingering unforgiveness in your heart.

I meet many people coming out of broken relationships who find it very difficult not to wish disaster on their former spouse's next relationship. If this is prolonged and sustained, it reveals a truly damaged heart that needs to experience the freedom that forgiveness brings.

It is worth saying again that while we think in holding grudges we are harming others, the deepest harm is to ourselves.

3) Do you frequently speak negatively about someone?

Every time that certain someone's name comes up in a conversation, do negative words slip out from your lips? Do you find satisfaction in letting people know what you think of them?

Gossip, slander, and back biting are the unholy trinity of grudges and lingering anger. They do a fine job of revealing what is in our hearts towards someone.

In Matthew 12:34 Jesus said, "Out of an abundance of the heart, the mouth speaks."

What a great diagnostic! Jesus reveals a law at

work in our members – that whatever is in our heart in abundance will come flying out of our mouth sooner or later!

Key point: Do NOT let the enemy use what comes out of your mouth to condemn you, let the Holy Spirit use it to point you towards your need for healing!

4) Do you try to turn others against them?

An easy way to tell if you are holding on to an offense is to ask yourself, "Do I nurse, rehearse, and disperse what that person did to me?" "Do I take that pain into my lap each day and feed it?" "Do I replay what that person did to me over and over again in my mind?" "Do I tell everyone I know what they did to me?" If the answer to any or all of these questions is yes; that is called "nursing, rehearsing, and dispersing an offense."

I know it can be very difficult not to want to talk to others about your anger. Therefore, I am not talking about you sharing your painful thoughts with a counselor or pastor.

The difference is while processing things out, are you with someone who is pointing you towards wholeness and healing or are you recruiting more people into your "corner" for the fight?

You can always give your angry words to God so you don't give them to someone you shouldn't. Perhaps record those angry words in your prayer journal, tell your Heavenly Father how you feel – He can handle them where certain people cannot.

Chapter 7:

Christ: The Source of Forgiveness

The congregation at Grace Church has heard me say many times, "Receiving is the first law of life." In other words, there is a law at work that human beings cannot give away something they do not first receive and possess.

We see this law in the scripture, "We love **because** God first loved us." So how do we become empowered to love others? By receiving God's love for us. Jesus accentuates the same principle in John 13:34 when He says, "Love one another **just as I love you**." So many miss the key component of this statement, which is to discover first how much He loves us!

Applying this principle to forgiveness works much better than my exhorting you to "Get tough and go muster up some forgiveness." I will instead ask you to begin accepting the magnitude of Christ's forgiveness for you first!

<u>In order for a human to truly forgive, we must first become keenly aware of the riches and wealth of forgiveness we have been GIVEN in Christ and receive those riches!</u>

You may have noticed in John 15 that Jesus Christ calls you a "branch." I don't know a whole lot about what branches do, but I am certain they do one thing: Receive. Do any branches you know stress, strain, or strive to bear fruit? Neither do I!

I also know branches are not self-generative, meaning they do not produce anything in and of themselves. Branches only display what comes *through* them from their source.

<u>Through basic reasoning then, we conclude forgiveness must first come to you before it can come through you.</u>

This is where I have great news! Let's look again at Ephesians 4:31-32.

"31 Let all bitterness, wrath, anger, clamor, and evil speaking be put away from you, with all malice. 32 And be kind to one another, tenderhearted, forgiving one another, <u>just as God in Christ forgave you."</u>

Did you see it? We are charged by the Apostle Paul to forgive JUST AS GOD IN CHRIST FORGAVE US. That is past tense. <u>That means forgiveness is not yours to be earned or deserved, it's yours to be accepted and shared</u>.

"Well Pastor Steve, I just don't deserve to be forgiven." I won't argue with that, but can you at least recognize how much of the Bible itself was written by and through former murderers, adulterers, and the like? Look at David, Moses, and Paul! Those guys have many skeletons in their closet. You need to stop thinking <u>so</u> <u>much</u> of your mistakes and <u>so</u> <u>little</u> of the wealth of God's forgiveness given to you in Christ!

Colossians 3:13 proclaims the same truth, "Bear with each other and forgive one another if any of you has a grievance against someone. <u>Forgive as the Lord forgave you.</u>"

Forgiveness can only be extended and given to others once it is received from God. Only once forgiveness comes TO the branch can it flow freely THROUGH the branch. Jesus Christ Himself and His Holy Spirit came in you the day you were saved and brought that supply of forgiveness with Him! You have it!

Let me ask you these questions according to
what we just read in Ephesians and Colossians:

1) Just how forgiven are you?

2) Just how cleansed are you?

3) Was Jesus Christ not sufficient for the
   removal of all your transgressions?

4) Why does Jesus not come down from
   heaven and die on the cross again every
   time you stumble?

5) Would God's Spirit even be living inside
   you at this moment if you weren't
   completely cleansed of all sin?

Truthful and honest answers to each of those
questions should reveal the magnitude and
fullness of Christ's work of forgiveness on the
cross.

So isn't it possible out of the tremendous
pardon which you have received, perhaps
considering releasing someone else's debt is not
as far out of reach as you might think?

Isn't it now possible with Christ supplying unlimited, once for all forgiveness to you, that you can be empowered to forgive yourself and others? I certainly think so.

The Outrageous Adequacy of Christ's Sacrifice

If you look at the Old Testament sacrifices for sin, there is an incredible foretelling of the completeness and totality of our forgiveness before God as His children.

People in the Old Testament brought sacrifices according to their means not according to the magnitude of their transgression. In other words, based on the sacrifice that was brought to the temple gate, one couldn't tell whether a person's sin was a lie (small sacrifice like a turtle dove) or adultery (big sacrifice like a bull). There was no such distinction made.

When the worshipper brought their sacrifice to God, no matter what they had done, no matter how big their sin was, not one time did the priest examine the worthiness of the individual bringing the sacrifice! Every time the priest examined the worthiness of the sacrifice itself! And when he found the sacrifice pure, acceptable, and holy, the worshipper walked away totally free from sin, cleansed, and in right relationship with God!

Bring that type and shadow to the New Testament. I don't care who you are, what you've done, or how many times you've done it; God is not examining your worthiness but rather the worthiness of the ONE HE sacrificed and offered for you – Jesus Christ! It is in Him alone you are forgiven, cleansed, and made right with God!

In John 13:8, as Jesus is preparing to WASH the disciples feet, Peter pipes up to Jesus, "You shall never wash my feet!" Jesus answered him, "If I do not WASH YOU, you have no part with Me." Notice it is Christ who must do the washing, it is Christ's sacrifice that cleanses. Even if Peter washed Jesus' feet until the end of time, his efforts towards Christ cannot make him clean! This is because it is we who need to be cleansed not Jesus. The only way we are cleansed is through Christ's offering on our behalf, and this offer has been made!

Chapter 8:

You Gotta Love Hebrews!

This chapter features one of my favorite books in all of Scripture. I want to show you, with the Holy Spirit's help, some amazing passages out of Hebrews that can change your entire perception of forgiveness and sin consciousness. Let's dig in!

Hebrews 9:11-14 says, "But Christ came as High Priest of the good things to come, with the greater and more perfect tabernacle not made with hands, that is, not of this creation. 12 Not with the blood of goats and calves, but with His own blood <u>He entered the Most Holy Place once for all, having obtained for us an eternal redemption</u>. 13 For if the blood of bulls and goats and the ashes of a heifer, sprinkling the unclean, sanctifies for the purifying of the flesh, 14 <u>how much more shall the blood of Christ,</u> who through the eternal Spirit offered Himself without spot to God, <u>cleanse your conscience from dead works to serve the living God?"</u>

Hebrews 10:1-2 adds, "For the law, having a shadow of the good things to come, and not the very image of the things, can never with these same sacrifices, which they offer continually year by year, <u>make those who approach perfect.</u> 2 For then would they not have ceased to be offered? <u>For the worshipers, once purified, would have had no more consciousness of sins.</u>

Hebrews 10:11-18 says, "Every priest stands ministering daily and offering repeatedly the same sacrifices, which can never <u>take away sins.</u> 12 <u>But this Man (Christ), after He had offered one sacrifice for sins forever,</u> <u>sat down at the right hand of God,</u> 13 from that time waiting till His enemies are made His footstool. 14 <u>For by one offering He has perfected forever those who are being made holy.</u> 15 But the Holy Spirit also witnesses to us; for after He had said before, 16 "This is the covenant that I will make with them after those days, says the Lord: I will put My laws in their hearts, and in their minds I will write them," 17 "<u>Their sins and their lawless deeds I will remember no more.</u>" 18 <u>Now where there is remission of sin, there is no longer an offering for sin.</u>"

Those are some stout, stout passages! Let's break down a few of the key verses:

Hebrews 9, Verse 12 – Christ came "once for all" regarding cleansing of sin, and His blood purchased for us an "eternal redemption" --not some temporary fix that you must keep up payments on.

Hebrews 10, Verse 1 & 2 – We see here two characteristics of what the Old Testament sacrifices could NOT produce in the worshippers: 1) It could not make them perfect. 2) It could not take away their sin consciousness.

What the author is saying however is that these two traits will belong to the worshippers once a sacrifice is offered "once for all" but not until then. Well, Christ is that final Sacrifice! So rejoice my friend, by His one offering you have been made perfect and can live no more in sin consciousness but in God consciousness!

Hebrews 10, Verse 11 - The blood of bulls and goats could not "take away" your sin, just cover it; but the blood of Jesus Christ takes away your sin. John the Baptist announced this wonderful news in John 1:29, "Behold, the Lamb of God who <u>takes away</u> the sin of the world."

All that bloodshed in the Old Covenant could not take away sin, nor make the worshipper perfect, nor cleanse the worshippers conscience, nor make the worshipper a brand new creation; but Jesus Christ the Lamb of God provided all that and more!

<u>Hebrews 10, Verse 12</u> – Jesus Christ offers ONE sacrifice for sins FOREVER. There is no other way for sins to be forgiven. <u>God has always used a blood based/sacrifice based economy for forgiveness; not an "I'm so sorry Lord" based economy; not an "I'll never do it again Lord" based economy; not an "I'll confess every sin I've ever committed" based economy.</u>

So many people struggle with forgiveness, both Christian and non-Christian alike, because they have never seen how forgiven they are! It would be hard for any branch to give out or supply something they did not perceive they possessed or had been supplied to them.

Also in Verse 12 – Notice Christ "sat down" after offering Himself as THE sacrifice for sin. First of all, no priest in history had ever offered Himself on behalf of the people or secondly, sat down after ministering a sacrifice and offering in God's Presence. Why did Jesus sit down? He was simply proving there was NO more work to be done for mankind's cleansing! "It is finished!"

Hebrews 10, Verse 14 – We see here by ONE offering Christ "has perfected forever" (that is past tense), those who are being made holy. While it's true you are still a work in progress in your mind and body (your spirit man is perfect), Christ has secured your forgiveness once for all.

Hebrews 10, Verse 17 & 18 – One of the terms of the New Covenant is that God will "remember our sins no more!" And it's such a complete offering for forgiveness, verse 18 says there is no more offering for sin! That means no more make up jobs for sin; no more penance for sin. Now I would say that makes you very forgiven in Christ and empowered by His Spirit and His forgiveness to forgive others.

Three proofs I know you're forgiven today as a born again Christian:

Proof #1 – God is living inside of you by His Holy Spirit! He talks to you and fellowships with you from within, right? <u>He wouldn't be living in you right now if He had not eradicated your sin issue.</u> Check out the Scriptures. God is incredibly Holy, right? He doesn't have any track record of living in or inhabiting unholy temples, yet He lives in you right now!

In John 14:16 Jesus said of the Holy Spirit, "He will abide with you forever." He does not say, "He will abide with you until you mess up." Sometimes I think when Christians say to God, "I just wanna be close to you," all of Heaven shouts back, "Hey, He's inside of you!"

Proof #2 – Jesus doesn't come down here and die every time you make a mistake. If Jesus' blood was not enough, would not the sacrifices and offerings for sin have continued?

Proof #3 – I know you're forgiven as a born again Christian because Jesus didn't just die for you, He died AS you.

Galatians 2:20 and Romans 6:6 both say *you* have been crucified *with* Christ. This makes perfect sense in God's economy, by the way. What's the wages of sin? Death. Have you ever sinned? Yes. In fact, you were born into sin through Adam. <u>So in a very just and fair act at the cross, you were tried, found guilty, and sentenced for your sin (in Christ).</u> Your sentence was of course death and Jesus Christ in His great love for you allowed the execution of your sentence to be carried out on Him! He effectively put the old sinful you to death on the cross by "drawing all men unto Himself when He was lifted up."

Romans 6:7 gloriously adds, "Whoever has died has been freed from sin." Congratulations, your death sentence was accomplished in the body of Jesus Christ! When He died, so did the old you because you've been, "crucified with Christ!" This means you are free to be "born again" and raised anew with Christ. You can no longer be tried for your past, because your judgment was *justly* poured out on you in Christ. You are now free to receive the new birth and serve God freely with a clean and clear conscience and a brand new heart, nature, and spirit.

Now if that doesn't light your fire, your wick is probably wet. If that doesn't empower you towards releasing someone from their debt to you, I'm not sure you have grasped the magnitude of how forgiven you are.

Forgiveness is supernatural. I could never ask you to go extend someone forgiveness without inviting you to first receive forgiveness from your Source, Jesus Christ.

Ephesians 1:7 says, "In Him we have redemption through His blood, the forgiveness of sins, according to the riches of His grace…"

Colossians 1:13-14 says, "He has delivered us from the power of darkness and conveyed us into the kingdom of the Son of His love, 14 in whom we have redemption through His blood, the forgiveness of sins."

The whole of the New Covenant is that God has unequivocally offered you His forever forgiveness! The only requirement? Receive it, believe it, and treat others like it's true!

Let's Talk Truth!

You know my place in your life as a pastor and an author? To simply encourage you to live like you're forgiven. To live like what God did for you actually happened! And here's the crazy part: It's true whether you believe it or not. It actually happened whether you think it did or not; so I suggest you and every other human on this planet believe it.

We're such funny creations at times. We think just because we don't believe something is true, it's not true. Well, the truth is that truth was here long before we got here and truth will be here long after we are gone. We are not God. We do not determine the truth; we only get to discover the truth. Once we do, if we will dance with the truth and join ourselves to it, it sets us free (See John 8:32).

<u>You will always struggle in forgiving others, forgiving yourself, and battling offense if you don't find peace over how forgiven you are in Christ.</u>

You may say, "But what about the sins I haven't committed yet?" When Christ died for the complete remission of your sin, you weren't even born yet, so every one of your sins He eradicated were future sins.

Don't believe a lie. Don't spend your whole life trying to earn something that's already been offered to you freely and in totality by God Himself.

Simply put, you're either operating on a works-based, you-centered forgiveness; or a blood-based, Christ-centered forgiveness. Doesn't it make sense, considering how holy Almighty God is, that HIS offering for sin would be the only acceptable offering?

Ever since Genesis, the enemy has always tempted man to try and become something God already says He is.

- Genesis 3. God makes man in His image; yet Satan tempts man to "be like God."

- Matthew 4. Jesus IS the Son of God yet is tempted with, "If you are the Son of God, command these stones to become bread." In other words, prove it by working independently of God.

- Romans 10. Jewish believers are made the righteousness of God in Christ yet are tempted to establish a "righteousness of their own."

- Present day. The believer is totally forgiven in Christ yet is tempted to find forgiveness through remorse, confession, works, or penance. Our forgiveness came through Christ alone, no additives or preservatives!

Pastor Steve Eden

Chapter 9:

Confronting and Combatting Feelings of Resentment

Psalm 147:3 says, "He heals the brokenhearted and binds up their wounds."

Many times our emotions can be relentless in their pursuit to dominate us. The first thing I want you to know is that Christ is near the broken hearted. He understands your pain. He is touched by your grief. He has compassion for you and great grace as well to carry you until you are lifted from the place you are in.

There are many people I have met who struggled overcoming the feelings or pain that a betrayal or breach of trust can cause. I have learned though, that sometimes actions of forgiveness can really empower us towards feelings of forgiveness.

In this chapter, let's explore some practical ways to COMBAT those "feelings" that try to come upon us from time to time even though we believe we have forgiven.

1) Celebrate your forgiveness before God each morning.

Let God's forgiveness toward you be a conscious thought you carry with you each day. What empowerment to possess an attitude of gratitude for God's mercies that are new each morning! It's hard to grudge on someone and give way to negative emotions while praising God for how forgiven you are! It's hard to carry offenses around when you know in your heart you didn't get what you <u>deserved</u>, but rather what God <u>desired</u> for you.

Psalm 103:1-5 says, "Bless the Lord, O my soul; And all that is within me, bless His holy name! 2 <u>Bless the Lord, O my soul, And forget not all His benefits: 3 Who forgives all your iniquities</u>, Who heals all your diseases, 4 Who redeems your life from destruction, Who crowns you with lovingkindness and tender mercies, 5 Who satisfies your mouth with good things, so that your youth is renewed like the eagle's.

This is a liberating passage to begin each day!

A very good friend of mine, Pastor Lee Armstrong, told me he begins every morning with a simple prayer that includes, "Father, because I am forgiven, I make the decision right now to forgive anyone that harms or hurts me today." He said he doesn't want to wait around until he's in the heat of a moment with someone and then try to renew his mind to do the right thing.

Colossians 2:13-14 says that at the cross Jesus purchased your certificate of debt and the record of your sin, and wiped it clean. So when the accuser comes to accuse you, he finds no evidence. I believe God wants you to remember, when you're tempted to tally up the wrongs on someone's certificate of debt they owe you, that He wiped your certificate clean!

Again, that was Jesus' point in Matthew 18:33 when He said to the unforgiving servant, "Should you not have shown mercy to him as I showed mercy to you?"

It is impossible to be married without having a spouse hurt or disappoint you, but please remember what your certificate of debt looks like! It is impossible to go to church with other Christians and minister together without someone hurting or disappointing you, so please remember what your certificate of debt looks like!

2) Find a safe place to dump your trash.

Because there are times when our emotions try to get the best of us, it is important we find a good, objective person who will point us toward wholeness rather than feed our ill-will.

God is certainly a good One to start with. Get yourself a prayer journal and write to Him expressively how you are feeling. As I mentioned before, He definitely can handle your 'strong' words, and then point you towards healing as well.

Other than confiding in God, perhaps there is a close, mature, Godly friend, or a small group leader at your church, or a pastor on staff that can remain unbiased. Make no mistake about it – many times we need a place to process and vent our wounded emotions.

A friend who really loves you is not going to urge you to nurse, rehearse, and disperse your grudge to other people. They will be understanding, empathetic, and compassionate; but they will also say, "I am so sorry that happened to you, but we need to make sure we let ALL bitterness, wrath, and anger be put away from you."

Jesus said in Luke 17:1, "Opportunities for offense will come..." so we need to make sure we have a safe place to heal.

3) Meet each invading resentment with a prayer!

1 Peter 3:8-12 says, "Finally, all of you be of one mind, having compassion for one another; love as brothers, be tenderhearted, be courteous; 9 not returning evil for evil or reviling for reviling, but on the contrary blessing, knowing that you were called to this, that you may inherit a blessing. 10 <u>For "He who would love life and see good days, Let him refrain his tongue from evil, And his lips from speaking deceit. 11 Let him turn away from evil and do good; Let him seek peace and pursue it.</u> 12 For the eyes of the Lord are on the righteous, And His ears are open to their prayers; But the face of the Lord is against those who do evil."

<u>Every time that person or circumstance arises in in your mind accompanied by negative emotions, I want you to release a prayer.</u>

And your prayer is not to be, "God get them! God teach them a hard lesson! God take them out! God punish them! Or smite them Oh Mighty Smiter!"

Pray this way, "Father, I pray they get what you desire for their life and not what they deserve; because that's what you did for me."

I think it is a good idea that our prayers should be Christian prayers. Verse 12 above says God does not get in line with evil doers. God does not and cannot answer prayers that are not Christ-like prayers. When Jesus said, "Whatever you ask the Father in My Name, He will do…"-- He is saying whatever you ask in His stead, in His character, or in His nature, the Father will do. He is not saying J-E-S-U-S is some kind of magic wand we tag our prayers with to get God to do what we want.

4) Do something good for the person with whom you feel bitterness.

Romans 12:17-18 says, "Repay no one evil for evil. Have regard for good things in the sight of all men. 18 If possible, as much as depends on you live peaceably with all men."

Romans 12:21 adds, "Do not be overcome by evil, but overcome evil with good."

As Christians, we often get opportunity to reveal how our hearts are different from the world. One of the ways we demonstrate that difference is by fighting evil with good, hate with love, ill-will with goodwill, and unrighteous behavior with righteous behavior.

Acting kindly to someone who has really hurt you or injured a loved one can be difficult at times, but I have found over and over again that acts of forgiveness can lead to feelings of forgiveness.

My friend Abbie was such an excellent example of this as you will read in Chapter 10.

A very similar story to Abbie's happened with one of the ladies I work with here at Grace Church. For the sake of privacy, I will call her name Cathy.

There was a woman Cathy did not like very much because she had caused some problems in her marriage, but the Lord asked Cathy to buy this woman a gift and personally deliver it!

Of course she balked sternly at first but eventually wanted to do what the Lord had asked.

Cathy thought it was so amazing that when she delivered the gift to this woman, the woman cried—then they even prayed together afterwards! Totally supernatural! Cathy said as soon as she offered her gift to the woman, all her ill feelings towards her vanished!

It is hard to have an <u>enemy</u> if you have no <u>enmity</u> (hate). Martin Luther said, "Be too glad and too great a person to be the enemy of any man." E. Stanley Jones said, "Be so pre-occupied with goodwill, there is no room in your heart for ill-will."

Good actions often CAN lead to good feelings!

5) Do not say "I don't like that person," say "There are things I don't like about that person."

In doing so, you separate the value of the person from their performance. We do the same thing with our children (hopefully) every time they make a mistake!

Your child's performance on Tuesday may have been a "two," but their value to you and to God is still a "ten." This is because performance does not determine human value, our value was determined by the One who made us!

So many times we base our value and identity on how we behave. We do a big piece of stupid and think, "Well, God could never love me," but God knows your value and identity are not based on what you do or did. They are based on who He created you to be!

Keep in mind also that you "war not with flesh and blood" (Ephesians 6:12). Remember, the same enemy who messes with you to hurt others messes with others to hurt you.

6) **Weigh the number of their transgressions against you with the number of your transgressions against God.**

Perhaps you remember Peter's infamous question to Jesus, "How many times should we forgive someone who wrongs us? Seven times?" Jesus remarkably said, "Not just seven times but seventy times seven."

Maybe you're like—"That can't be! Is He serious?" Yet oh how many times has the Lord done that for us? If God is only a God of "second chances," we are all in big trouble because we've blown it many more times than just twice! He is a God of multiple second chances where we are concerned.

Many people have trouble releasing the debts of others because they are not keenly aware of how big their debt was before God. This was definitely the Pharisees' undoing.

In John 9:41 Jesus said to them, "If you would admit you are blind, you would have no sin; but because you say, "We see," therefore your sin remains."

The Pharisees had a difficult time recognizing they needed God's grace as much as the next guy. If they could have only seen their own transgressions before God, it would have shown up in how they treated others.

In Luke 7:36-50, we read the story of a woman who washed Jesus' feet with perfume and dried His feet with HER OWN HAIR!

In verse 47, Jesus said her love for Him revealed how forgiven she believed she was. She was not lavishly worshipping Jesus with perfume <u>to be forgiven</u>; she was worshipping Him because <u>she knew she had been forgiven</u>!!

The principle is this: The revelation of our own forgiveness produces love in our hearts. When we really know we have been forgiven before God, it shows up in how we love Jesus and others. Forgiven people typically forgive.

<u>Christians who believe they didn't get what they deserved from God typically don't go around giving other people what they deserve!</u>

If you're struggling to love others, don't ask God to make other people more "loveable;" ask Him to take you to the next level of knowing how loved and forgiven you are!

That is why when you walk daily in faith that God loves you and has forgiven ALL your sin, it gets easier to love unlovely people. You begin to realize, "Hey, God loves me because He's so good-- not because I'm always so good." You recognize, "Hey, God loves me because He's so pure-- not because I'm always so pure." With that, we begin to do the same – treat others how God treats us. (This was Jesus' "new command" in John 13:34.)

Jesus has always had a valid argument that it is hard for us to justify not forgiving others when we have been forgiven of so much.

All along, Jesus has wanted to love you into loving and forgive you into forgiving. Will you allow Him to do that?

If your loving others never accomplishes what you hoped it would, you have still fulfilled your purpose because you've become a loving person. There is no higher call than that! There is no higher Christian maturity than that!

7) **Let God redeem it!**

Whatever injustice you have suffered, let it become seed in your hand. The moment it turns useable and redemptive, it loses all of its anger, guilt, and shame.

Psalm 126:5-6 says, "Those who sow in tears Shall reap in joy. 6 He who continually goes forth weeping, gathering seed for sowing, Shall doubtless come again with rejoicing, Bringing his sheaves with him."

Verse 6 says those times we are weeping, we are also gathering seed for sowing to help others. God wastes nothing! Everything furthers you and your development in Christ.

As stated earlier, not only can Christians stand everything that happens to us, we can use everything that happens to us! That is what makes us invincible.

We don't serve our past, our past serves us! I remember the Lord asking me if only my good deeds were useable to Him – or if He could use my past mistakes and sufferings to help people too. I was immediately convicted that I was hiding certain bad things I had done and only allowing Him to use the good things.

Romans 8:28 says, "And we know that God causes all things to work for the good of those who love him, who have been called according to his purpose."

You've been hurt and so have I. You've made big mistakes and so have I. Let's place them all in our Father's redemptive hands and start sowing good seed from it!

8) <u>Sow mercy.</u>

Why sow mercy when someone hurts you? Because one day you will be the one who needs mercy in human relationships!

If you're married, it is a good idea to sow mercy towards your spouse when they stumble because I assure you – your missteps are coming.

We all get that spirit of tit for tat and do unto others as they have done unto you, but that is NOT what the Bible says! Jesus said, "Do unto others AS you would have them do unto you."

Have you ever heard a 3 year old give a reason for hitting another child? It sounds like, "Well, he did it to me first." Do you see how immature that line of thinking is? Yet, I know many adults whose whole life is built on that concept.

That is not you. You are a new creation in Christ-- righteous, redeemed, truly holy, and full of the Life and Spirit of Christ.

9) <u>Let God be the judge!</u>

This is a good place to mention James 1:20 which says, "Human anger does not produce the righteousness of God."

Your Heavenly Father has far more information on why the person who hurt you actually hurt you than you do. He knows all that has gone into their life, their personality, and upbringing far more than you. Because of this, God is much better suited to judge matters, intents of the heart, and motives than you and I are.

1 Peter 2:21-23 says, "You were called, because Christ suffered for you, leaving you an example, that you should follow in his steps. 22 "He committed no sin, and no deceit was found in his mouth." 23 When they hurled their insults at him, he did not retaliate; when he suffered, he made no threats. <u>Instead, he entrusted himself to him who judges justly."</u>

Jesus entrusted Himself to the One who judges justly! He knew His Father was witness to all that was happening to Him; therefore, He did not defend or protect Himself, or plot revenge.

There was a teenager here in our area that we came to know through an assisted living home for troubled teens. This young man hated his dad. In his mind, and honestly in the mind of the world, he had many valid reasons for his hatred. He told us of the awful things his father had done to him and his sister, even treating them like literal dogs at one time.

One day a couple from Grace Church began ministering to the young man and simply asked if he would allow Jesus to share His perspective on the matter. The young man reluctantly said, "Yes."

As they began to pray together, the couple asked Jesus to bring healing to the young man. It was then the Lord began showing the teen how his dad himself had grown up without a father; and that his dad had experienced a tremendous amount of darkness and pain.

In that moment, the boy's countenance completely changed! He began to realize what all had gone into his dad's woeful and distorted view of what being a father meant. He went from outright anger with his dad to weeping for him! A tremendous burden came off of that young man that night and he has never been the same.

10) Ask Jesus what to do about your negative emotions and then do whatever He tells you to do.

John 2:5 says of Jesus, "His mother said to the servants, "Whatever He says to you, do it.""

You want some sound advice? There is not much better than what Mary suggests to the servants at the Cana Wedding.

This is how supernatural miracles happen; do whatever Jesus asks you to do. To the man with the withered hand in the temple Jesus said, "Stretch forth your hand," and when he did, his hand was healed.

When Peter saw Jesus on the water, he said, "Lord if it is you, bid me to come." Jesus said to Peter, "Come!" And so for at least a moment or two – Peter walked on water! There is always grace and power to carry out whatever Jesus asks us to do.

Jesus may say to you to fast for three days. He may say to pray for the person who hurt you. He may tell you to buy them a soda or bake them a pie. He may ask you to go to that person and offer peace just as He has asked so many other believers before you. The bottom line is this: whatever He says do – do it. He is inviting you to the supernatural!

In closing this list of how to combat feelings of resentment practically, please again remember; many times actions of forgiveness can lead to feelings of forgiveness. We are not always going to "feel" like doing the right things but if Jesus is asking it- you can bet there is life in it!

Chapter 10:

Blessed Abbie

I pray this book has blessed and enriched you. I pray it has challenged you to go deeper in allowing Christ's Spirit, Life, and character to be expressed through you. With that, I want to leave you with a wonderful testimony of goodness triumphing over tragedy, and of good will overtaking ill-will.

Many years ago I knew a very special woman in our congregation who I will name "Abbie." She has since gone on to be with Jesus, but I have shared her story many, many times to bring empowerment and healing to multiple people. Abbie had been coming to Grace Church for a while, had two precious children, and a heart full of genuine love for everyone – except, because of a variety of reasons, the father of those two children I mentioned. This is her story as she wrote it out some years ago:

"My ex-husband and I had a tumultuous relationship. It was full of mistrust, jealousy, and any bad emotion you can think of. He was physically and mentally abusive and I felt he was too hard on our children. When I finally got the courage to leave him, he actually took one of our children and I had no idea where they were! I harbored a lot of ill feelings toward him and I had sworn to myself that I would never forgive him for the pain and anguish I felt he had put me through.

After attending Grace Church for a while, Pastor Steve began a new series on the importance of forgiveness. He talked about how holding onto grudges and bitterness is very harmful to us, our well-being, and our bodies.

One morning during the message, God spoke to me about my ex-husband. I began to argue with God explaining to Him that I had every right to hold onto these feelings because my ex-husband did not deserve any forgiveness from me! He had put me through hell and I was not going to release him from that.

Well, the Lord was relentless and finally got me to go forward for prayer. As one of the pastors prayed with me, I cried like I haven't cried in a long time.

It was as if my tears rolling down my face were all the hateful feelings I had held onto for so long, and they were finally flowing out of me.

I not only forgave my ex-husband that day, but the Lord also prompted me to ASK MY EX-HUSBAND TO FORGIVE ME for holding on to all those awful and ill feelings I had toward him for the last several years!!

Following service that day, my next mission was to call my ex-husband and tell him what happened. He doesn't necessarily believe in God, but I can tell you he met Jesus inside of me that day!

I explained to him that at church that morning I had forgiven him for everything he had done to me. Then I asked him to please forgive me for harboring and also venting all the hatred and bitterness I had toward him. We both cried. Can you believe it? Then we talked with each other for about an hour after.

Nothing has been the same since that day. We are so much more civil to each other and he actually calls me and I talk with him about his problems with his girlfriend.

This is something that ten years ago, I would never have seen happening, but it has and I have so much more peace now!"

Abbie's story is such a triumph of the grace and power of God. It is such glaring evidence that all of us CAN FIND freedom through forgiveness! Abbie demonstrated once again the human body, heart, and mind are designed for peace and goodwill; never ill-will. Her testimony is such a manifestation of Jesus' desire that His Father's Kingdom would come and His will would be done on Earth as it is in Heaven. After all, are there any grudges in Heaven? No. Are there any offended people in Heaven? Nah, I don't think so – simply because he who the Son sets free is free indeed!

ABOUT THE AUTHOR

At the age of 20, Steve Eden had a personal encounter with Jesus Christ while attending Northeastern (Oklahoma) State University. Feeling burned out and like a complete failure as a young Christian, it was in that encounter Jesus told him, "Steve, I love you because of who I am not because of what you do. So I invite you to live the rest of your life from My love and not for it."

From that time on, with the Holy Spirit's guidance, Steve has been on a journey to bring himself and others out of performance based Christianity and into an intimate, vibrant, present tense relationship with his Lord, Savior, and Best Friend Jesus Christ.

Made in the USA
Lexington, KY
29 December 2018